SCHIRMER'S LIBRARY
OF MUSICAL CLASSICS

Vol. 1125

F RANZ S CHUBERT

Impromptus

For the Pianoforte

Edited and Fingered by
G. BUONAMICI

ISBN 978-0-7935-5201-6

G. SCHIRMER, Inc.

DISTRIBUTED BY

7777 W. BLUEMOUND RD. P.O. BOX 13819 MILWAUKEE, WI 53213
Printed in the U.S.A. by G. Schirmer, Inc.

CONTENTS

Four Impromptus.

Edited and fingered by
G. BUONAMICI.

F. SCHUBERT. Op. 90.

Allegro molto moderato. (♩ = 108.)

1.

Printed in the U.S.A. by G. Schirmer, Inc.

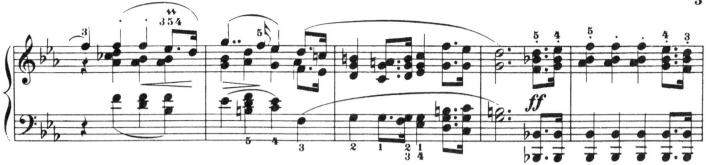

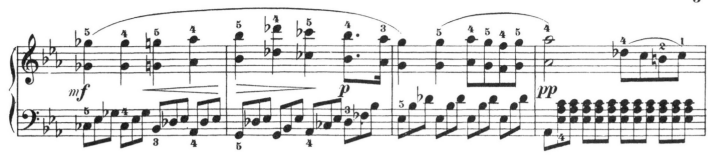

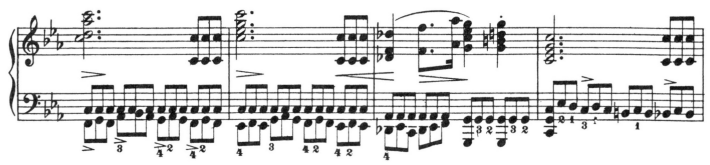

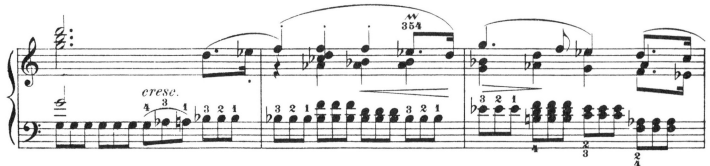

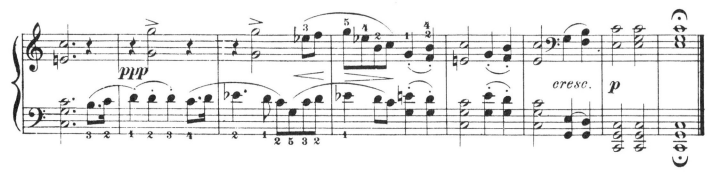

Four Impromptus.

Edited and fingered by
G. BUONAMICI.

F. SCHUBERT. Op. 90.

Allegro. ($\lozenge \cdot = 69$.)

2.

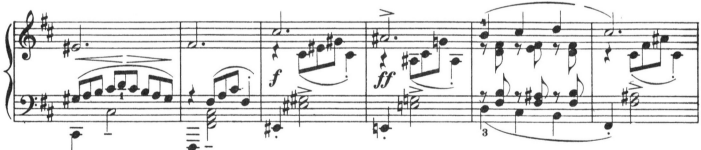

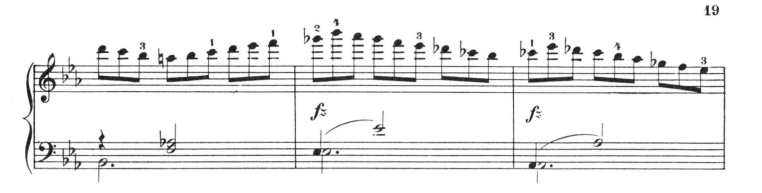

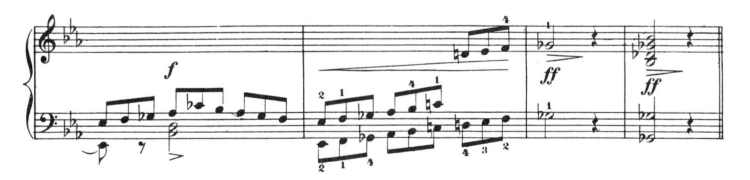

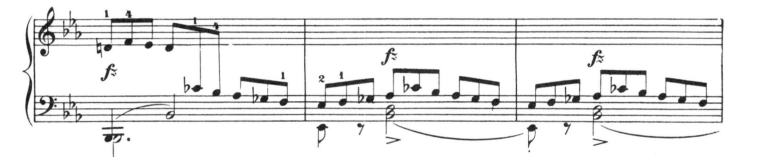

Coda.

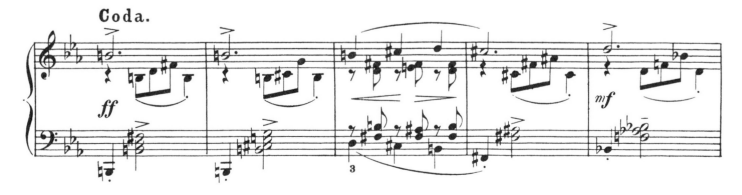

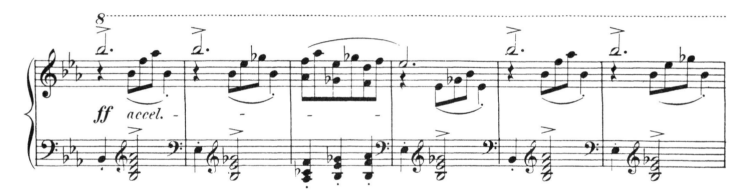

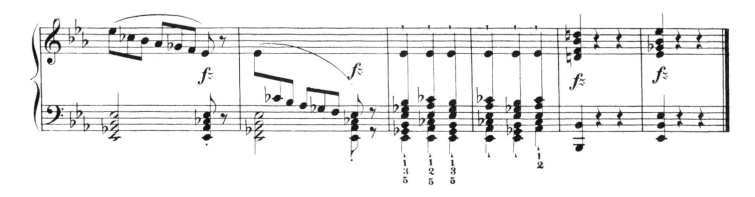

Four Impromptus.

Edited and fingered by
G. BUONAMICI.

F. SCHUBERT. Op. 90.

Andante mosso. (♩ = 84)

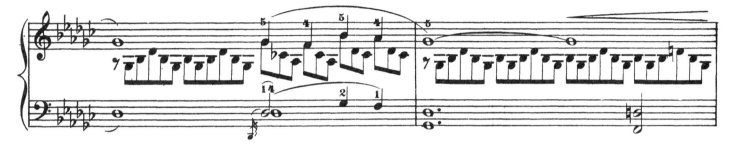

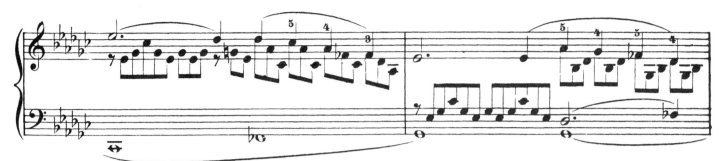

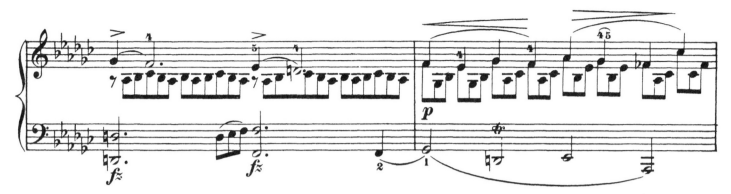

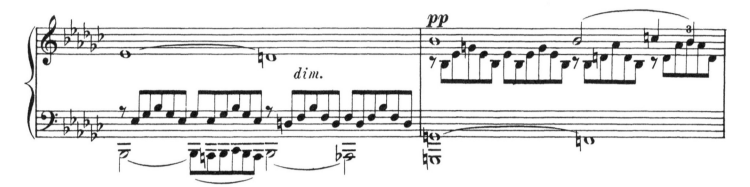

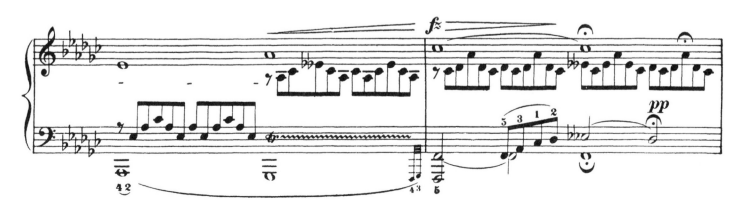

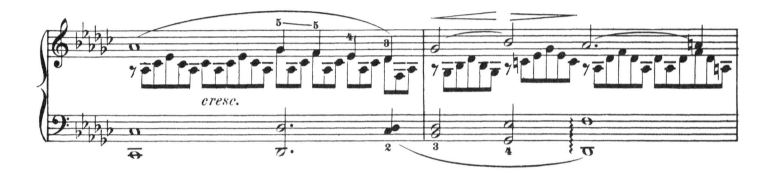

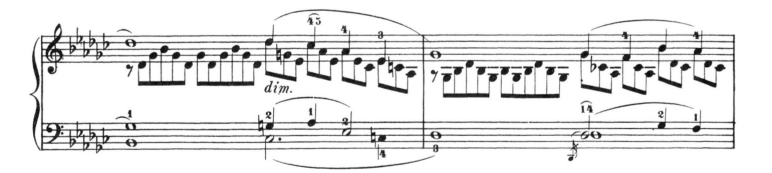

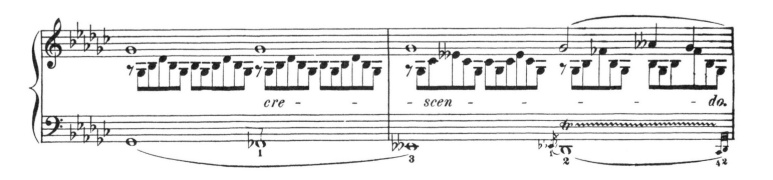

Four Impromptus.

Edited and fingered by
G. BUONAMICI.

Allegretto. ($\bullet$ = 144.)

F. SCHUBERT. Op. 90.

4.

pp

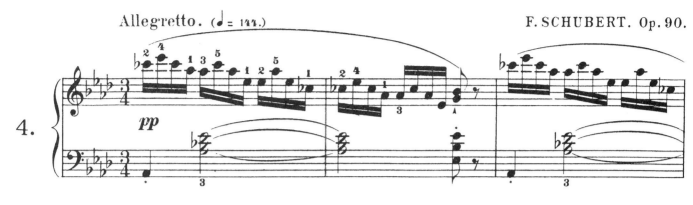

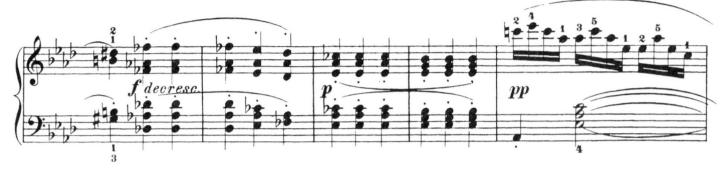

a) The measures from (a) to (b), and from (c) to (d), may be omitted.

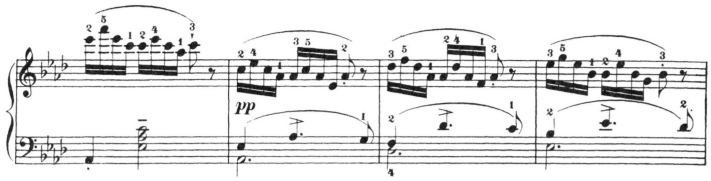

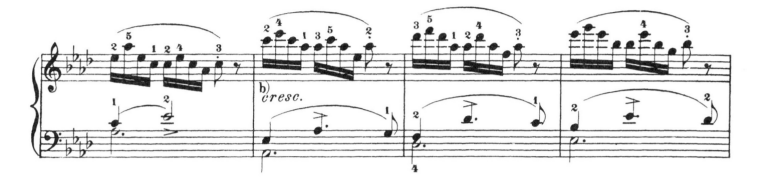

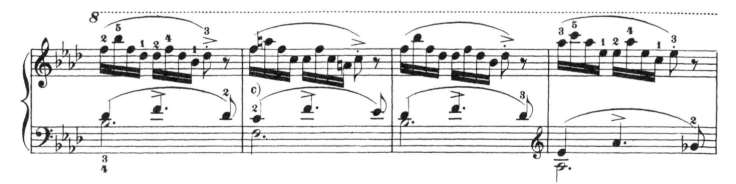

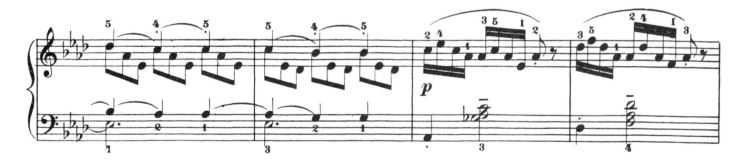

May also be played thus:

a) See note on Second Page.

May be played
as above.

etc.

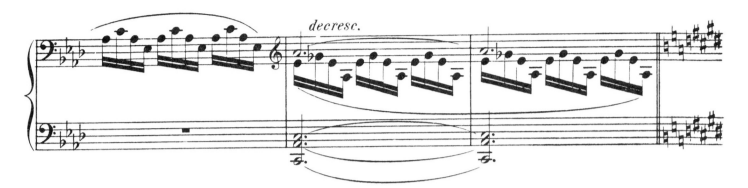

Trio.

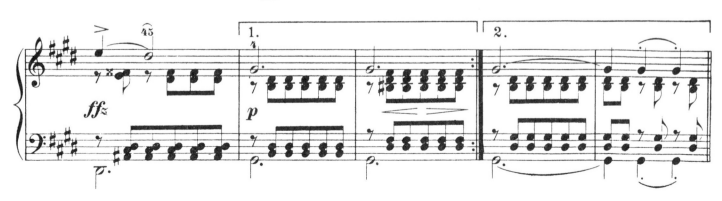

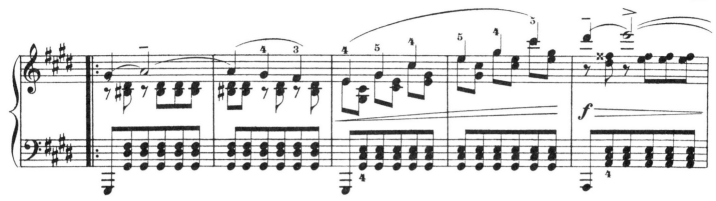

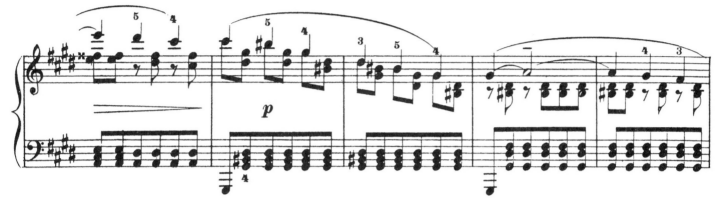

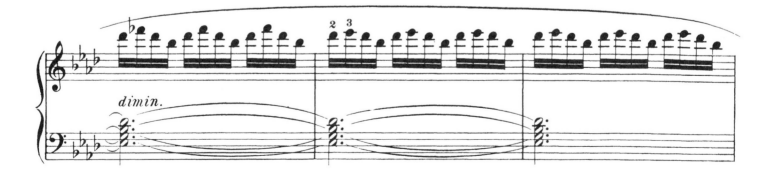

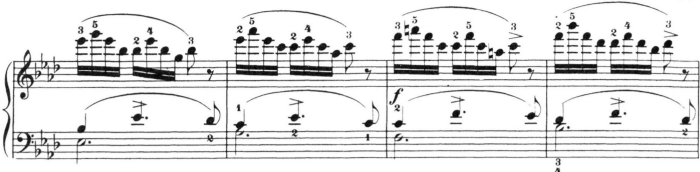

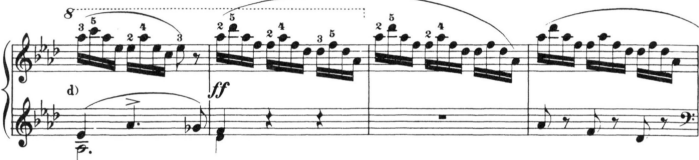

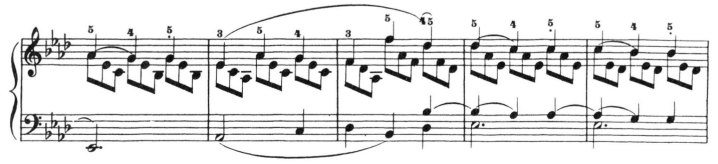

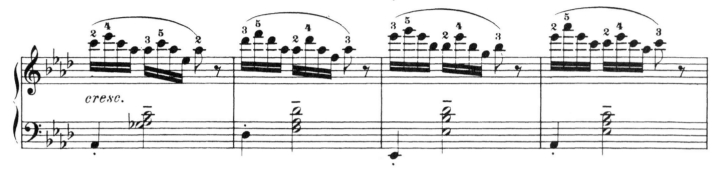

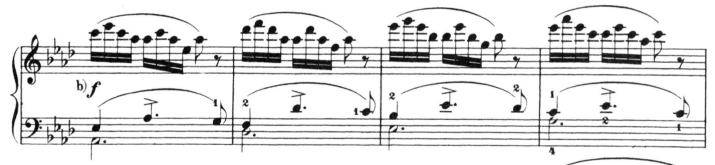

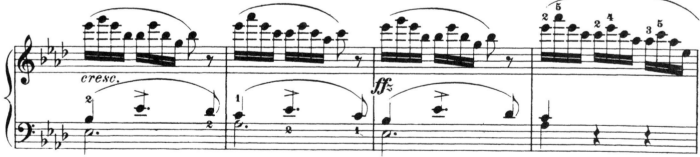